DREAM

Dream: Walk in Your God-Given Purpose

W. Ray Martinez

TruMission.com

U.S.A.

To Lilli and Will

CONTENTS

When you let the Holy Spirit paint dreams and a vision upon the canvas of your heart, a picture will emerge that will stagger your imagination and test your faith.

- ROBERT MORRIS

DREAMS

A Genie in a Bottle

You know the drill.

If you happen upon a genie in a bottle,
you get three wishes,
and no wishing
for more wishes.

Early in my walk with Christ, I thought I had
stumbled upon a genie.

"Take delight in the Lord, and he will give you the
desires of your heart" (Psalm 37:4, NLT).

There it is!

All I need to do is delight in the Lord
and boom—I get my wishes!

It took me a few years to fully understand what this
verse meant, and it wasn't about granting wishes.

Born for This

God placed a dream inside each of us before we took our first breaths. It is the purpose He had in mind when He created us.

This plan is locked within our hearts, waiting to emerge.

When we enter His presence, we come to understand something profound: God's not a genie in a bottle.

He desires much more than granting wishes;
He desires an authentic relationship with you. It's from this relationship with Him that the plan begins to unfold.

As you draw close to Him through spiritual discipline, the dream within you will awaken and the cry of the desire to fulfill your purpose will become more real.

There's a dream in you waiting to be born, and there's a world counting on you to give birth to it.

A Dreamer's Story

Perhaps the greatest story of a dreamer can be found in the life of a man named Joseph, whose story stretches from Genesis 37 to 50. A brief overview of his story will serve us well as we look toward his example.

Joseph was the youngest child of Jacob and was favored by his father over all his brothers. It was Jacob's love for Joseph that incited jealousy amongst his brothers.

Through a series of dreams, God began to show Joseph the destiny that awaited him. Excited by the future, he shared his dream with his family, who were all but enthusiastic for him. His dreams only intensified the envy and disdain his brothers had toward him. After an abandoned plot for murder, his brothers settled on selling Joseph into slavery and convincing their father that his favorite son was dead.

Enslavement was only the beginning of the tragic road that lay in front of Joseph.

Yet through every seeming setback, Joseph held on to the dream God had given him and, in the end, saw it all come to pass.

Joseph's story is a fascinating tale of what it means to hold on to a dream even when it looks like the odds are stacked against you.

Throughout this book, we will explore Joseph's life, his challenges, and his dreams. My prayer is that you will discover your own narrative in the life of this dreamer and dream big!

The Layout

The close of every chapter ends with an exercise meant to challenge you. I encourage you to get a pen and journal in hand.

Let's bring it to life!

Your mission is waiting.

Small beginnings are the launching pad
to great endings.

- JOYCE MEYER

HUMILITY

There's Greatness in You

It may have diminished somewhere along the path,
but at the core of us all is
a desire to make a lasting impact.

We have all had big dreams before.

When we were children, we saw no limits to our
dreams; if we could imagine it,
we could do or be it.

It didn't matter how grandiose or wild our dreams
were, we believed in them without a shadow of a
doubt. We'd go to the moon or change the world
without batting an eye.

It's a beautiful thing to dream big,
and as children that's what we did best.

Unfortunately for many of us,
something in life
caused us to stop dreaming big.

What in the past caused you to stop dreaming?

His Progressive Plan

As Jesus was about to leave his disciples, he made this statement:

"But you will receive power when the Holy Spirit comes upon you. And you will be my witnesses, telling people about me everywhere—in Jerusalem, throughout Judea, in Samaria, and to the ends of the earth" (Acts 1:8, NLT).

Did you see the progression?

Jesus says they will expand from
their hometown,
their region,
their surrounding regions, and
then to the entire world.

God wants to take us to new heights in an
ever-increasing,
ever-expanding
mission of reaching our world for the cause of the Gospel.

God desires that we would inspire
as many as possible to embrace
His life-altering love and enter
His eternal Kingdom.

It has never been God's plan for us to settle for just good enough or the status quo. His plan for us has always been for greatness.

"Now all glory to God, who is able, through his mighty power at work within us, to accomplish infinitely more than we might ask or think" (Ephesians 3:20, NLT).

The Amplified Version adds more detail to the end of the verse: "...far over and above all that we (dare) ask or think (infinitely beyond our highest prayers, desires, thoughts, hopes, or dreams)."

If greatness is what God has in store for us, then we must ask ourselves one question: Are we cultivating a place of greatness that will endure beyond ourselves?
That place of greatness within us is a heart fueled by faith, a mind steadfast in the Lord, and a life ready to serve. How do we come to this place of greatness

that the Lord has called us to? By investing deeply in the spiritual disciplines.

Spiritual Disciplines

In our reduction-based culture that demands quick, cheap, and easy, we have lost a deep sense of what it means to practice spiritual discipline. In the disciplines, we discover intimate fellowship with God. Here are a few that will help in your journey with God:

- Study—God's Word is the foundation that we build upon. It is in His Word that we discover the truth of who He is and who we are in Him.

- Worship—It is no accident that music and song move and connect us. Worship is a gift that allows our spirits to quickly connect to the Lord and changes the atmosphere when applied.

- Prayer—At its roots, prayer is about communication connecting us to God. What an honor that the God of the universe is always ready to take our call.

- Fasting—While prayer connects us to God, times of fasting disconnect us from the world.

- Solitude—Especially for those of us who are extroverts, time alone can be uncomfortable, but in an overly connected world, it is precisely what we need at times to refresh.

- Fellowship—For those of us who are introverts, this one can be taxing; but just as we need time alone, we need time together to strengthen one another.

There are many more spiritual disciplines that you can practice.

For a more thorough list, I highly suggest Dallas Willard's book, *The Spirit of the Disciplines: Understanding How God Changes Lives*.

Giants Before Kings

As a young man, David worked in the fields faithfully tending to the needs of his father's sheep.

One day he heard the call of a familiar voice telling him to leave the area and hurry home.

Swiftly entering the door of his home, he realized something was different.

Had someone died?

Why were all his brothers standing with his father, and why was the prophet Samuel present?

Looking intently into his eyes, as if he had seen a flash of destiny before him, Samuel exclaimed, "It's him! The king."

Hardly able to catch his breath, David felt the warmth of oil flowing down his head as the prophet declared him king of Israel.

But the king didn't take
the throne the next day;
he was back caring for sheep.

Quite often, our anointing comes well before the
actualization of our dream.

Even though the dream has taken
root in our heart,
we are back to
caring for the sheep, so to speak.

There is still a period of time when we go about our
normal lives, but during this season,
we must
tend to and
nourish that
dream within us.

I Ought To

It can be easy to lose sight when we consume ourselves with what ought to be.

I "ought to be" the boss.

I "ought to be" in charge.

I "ought to be" the one.

Each of our journeys is heading in the direction of greatness, but they all begin at the same size: small.

The time will come when you take down giants and advance.

Don't lose the dream,
and likewise,
don't let the vision of the future become
a distraction in your present.

Hold on to the dream and live in the moment. God has given you a divine purpose—never let it go.

One day,
soon enough,
what is in your heart
will match what you hold in your hand,
but along the way are invaluable preparations.

Before David slew a giant and sat on a throne, he cared for sheep and fought lions and bears.

Humble Beginnings

I often think about the humble beginnings of Jesus. His journey could have begun anywhere.

In the lavish home of kings.

In the influential household of generals.

Amongst the wealthy families of His day.

But it was none of these that Jesus was born into. Instead, He chose to be delivered to an otherwise unknown teenage mother in a manger, of all places.

And the Scripture says, "Jesus grew in wisdom and in stature and in favor with God and all the people" (Luke 2:52, NLT). The fulfillment of Jesus's purpose didn't happen right away. We speak so much about

Jesus's redemptive work on the cross, and rightly so, but how often do you stop to consider the entire life He lived before that?

Jesus was a baby, child, and teenager. Then He worked as a young man, plying His father's trade. There was a long time where Jesus waited, prepared, and grew so that He could fulfill His purpose.

He didn't move until the time was right.

It's the same way for us. There's a time and place for our dream to bloom, and we must prepare ourselves as we eagerly await that day.

Every dream has a small beginning.

There is much to be gained in the humble beginnings of our journey on mission with God.

Embrace those humble beginnings and the life lessons you learn along the way.

They will serve you well on the day you step out into your glorious purpose.

Your Story

Abraham was one hundred years old and Sarah was ninety before they had their first child together.

Moses had a stuttering problem when God called him to stand before one of the greatest powers in the world and speak.

Gideon was a terrified wimp when God called him a warrior.

Peter was a failure who denied Christ before he became a leader in the early church.

History is filled with those who overcame adversity and excelled.

The ability to overcome gives birth to hope and challenge—hope that the possibility to become better is achievable; challenge in that excuses become eliminated.

For if one person can overcome life's obstacles to accomplish something great, then the door of opportunity opens for others.

All that you have been through in life is a preparation for your purpose in the mission God has called you to.

I want to be clear that God has never been working destruction in your life (John 10:10), but He can and will redeem the past for good (Romans 8:28).

Let those negative experiences and seasons of waiting in your life serve as fuel and inspiration to become everything God has destined you to become.

Your pains,
victories,
and even losses
all tell the story of where you came from and set the stage for what lies ahead.

Embrace all of them as you step into your unique role in this world.

Joseph's Beginnings

Joseph had a dream that inspired greatness in his life, but where he found himself early in the story was any place but that of success.

He began his journey working for his older brother (Genesis 37:2), a prospect far removed from his vision, but one rich with lessons that would be critical for the purpose in his life.

During this time, Joseph began to have dreams, ones that indicated Joseph would come to take a position of leadership and influence.

But Joseph was not there yet.

He was still a humble boy working the fields.

Even though his dream was still a long way off from coming to fruition,
Joseph was learning
humility,
work ethic,
and how to serve others—
all traits that would come to define his rule in Egypt.

Exercise: Timeline

In this first exercise, let's get a thirty-thousand-foot view of your life by laying out the best detailed timeline that you can. Looking at your life in this way can help you to more easily see the trajectory that God has placed you on. Here you can see how He has been preparing you for your dream. As you consider these things, think of ways that you can cultivate the seeds He has been planting within you.

Note: You may remember stuff later. Using index cards can help you move events around as you develop your timeline.

Birth	Graduated	Started Career	Married
1991	2015	2019	2020

Integrity is not a given factor in everyone's life. It is a result of self-discipline, inner trust, and a decision to be relentlessly honest in all situations in our lives.

- JOHN MAXWELL

INTEGRITY

First Things First

From the depths of our being,
we are challenged to walk with Christ into the mission
of helping others discover the life found in the risen
Savior. It is from those depths that
our true character will be revealed.

The fact is, if we are to do
anything of worth,
anything of greatness,
anything of value,
we must first have a firm
foundation of integrity.

We can easily fool ourselves into believing that we
will make the right choices along the way, but it's not
in the middle of the battle that we form our values;
values must be formed long before you take the
field, as the field will only reveal what has already
been shaped.

Most people never take the time to truly define the
values of their life,
and as a result,
there is a chasm between
desire and reality.

We will talk more about this soon, but for now, make up your mind that you will not go another day winging the core values of your life. Instead, from this day forward, choose to be intentional. When everything you do is aligned with your purpose, you will be putting your dream into action!

The Potter's Wheel

I've heard it said before that "you must not allow your talent to carry you to a place where your character cannot sustain you."

Look at the mental imagery of this next text:
"So I did as he told me and found the potter working at his wheel. But the jar he was making did not turn out as he had hoped, so he crushed it into a lump of clay again and started over" (Jeremiah 18:3-4, NLT).

Poetic, yes. Intense, even more so.

Jeremiah's vision of clay is a picture of our lives, and the potter is God. Sometimes we make a mess out of what He has entrusted us with. In these moments, the intense work of the potter requires the marring of the clay.

What does this mean?

It means there is work to be done for the Lord and that it won't always be
comfortable,
easy, or
pleasant.

It is in this sense that we lay down our life to God as a living sacrifice.

"Give your bodies to God because of all he has done for you. Let them be a living and holy sacrifice—the kind he will find acceptable. This is truly the way to worship him. Don't think you are better than you really are. Be honest in your evaluation of yourselves, measuring yourselves by the faith God has given us" (Romans 12:1, 3, NLT).

A sacrifice is only a sacrifice if it stays upon the altar. It is at the altar that change occurs in the sacrifice.

What was will no longer be.

Paul's words are meant to rescue our lives from selfish pursuits and realign them into God-sized plans.

Don't "Cretize"

If you want to understand what it means to walk in integrity, the Pauline epistles dubbed the pastoral letters are a great start.

In his letter to Titus, Paul charges his protégé to bring order to the church in Crete. A glimpse at the obstacles before Titus in implementing the charge is found in the latter part of chapter one.

In verses 12 and 13, Paul delivers a severe accusation against Crete, quoting one of their own prophets who denounced them as liars, evil, and lazy:
"Even one of their own men, a prophet from Crete, has said about them, 'The people of Crete are all liars, cruel animals, and lazy gluttons.' This is true. So reprimand them sternly to make them strong in the faith" (Titus 1:12-13).

Not withholding his own opinion, Paul declares that their prophet has spoken the truth about the Cretans' moral standards.

At first glance, Paul's accusation seems harsh; however, exploring the cultural setting reveals a history that has stigmatized the region.

The Cretans propagated a claim that Zeus was buried in their city, which was, of course, refuted. The depth of their deception led to the colloquial phrase "to *cretize*," which means to lie or cheat.

Be a Witness

In a region known for its dishonesty and lack of moral standards, Titus had the arduous task of developing leaders to advance the mission of God.

To this end, Paul places the onus of integrity upon young Titus, whereby his standard would bear witness to a better life found in Christ Jesus:

"You yourself must be an example to them by doing good works of every kind. Let everything you do reflect the integrity and seriousness of your teaching. Teach the truth so that your teaching can't be criticized. Then those who oppose us will be ashamed and have nothing bad to say about us" (Titus 2:7-8, NLT).

Notice that Paul does not have Titus withdraw from the secular world around him but boldly approach it through the power of Christ within.

Like Titus, we must boldly enter our world and forge a new way.

As we travel through this lived mission, we have an opportunity to exude the moral qualities that the world around us longs for. The plague of immorality is not new to this world; it has existed since the fall of humanity in Genesis.

The present age has seen its share of ethical downfalls and has desperately tried to address the issues with humanistic theories.

The remedy is found in those willing to do the hard work of cultivating God-shaped values such as
faith,
godly love, and
humility in their lives.

Conflicted

Are we living a life that brings honor to God? Listen to the powerful charge of Jesus:

"Let your good deeds shine out for all to see, so that everyone will praise your heavenly Father" (Matthew 5:16, NLT).

The words of the Savior are meant to reverberate in our actions. I will assume that we all hope our espoused values will be attested to in the fruit of our efforts.

But what do we do when there is a disconnect between our values and how we actually live our lives?

And straighter to the point, how do we even locate the disconnect?

Going back to the idea of doing the hard work up front, you can only acknowledge a disconnect when you have first established the parameters.

Consider your core values to be your factory reset mode if pressed. While exploring your values, I encourage you to make a list without first considering the length. In Exercise 2, you will be challenged to narrow down your values to three or four (of course, you can have more values).

Espoused vs. Actualized

The exercise at the end of this chapter is meant to assist you along the way, but for now, let's define two categories that will be essential in plotting your course.

The first is a look at the desired values of our lives that we hope present us as trustworthy and ethical.

The next category to consider is the actualized values in your life. Have you ever heard the phrase, "Do as I say, and not as I do"?

Actualized values are less about the saying and more about the doing part of our lives.

Locating the actualized values takes a great deal of introspective searching and humble acceptance.

This task will require you to get honest feedback from those you trust.

Ask—without defending yourself—what they see as your strengths and your weaknesses.

The person you are seeking counsel from needs to know that they can trust you to handle their feedback.

Humbly listen.

Once you have your desired values written down and have gathered insight from others, it's time to get alone and start the hard part.

You see, only you can answer the tough questions and intentions of your heart.

If you desire to locate a disconnect between your cherished values and your lived values, you will have to wrestle with the honesty of your heart.

Joseph's Character

Joseph learned the lesson of character early in his life. Though he was the youngest of his brothers, his father knew that he could count on Joseph to do what was right despite what immoral actions of his siblings (Genesis 37:2).

His character carried him to positions of honor and leadership because it was his character that sustained him despite persecution.

The forging of his character in the crucible of conflict would prove invaluable later in his life when his integrity would be put to the test by the brazen passion of Potiphar's wife.

Exercise: Value Setting

In the first column, list three to six values that are important to you. Keep in mind that these are the things you want to be known for.

In the third column, fill in your findings from the honest feedback you gathered to determine the present actualized values in your life.

The center column is a space for you to reflect. If your desired values perfectly match your actualized values, then use this section to develop action steps to reinforce your values. If they don't match, use the area to set goals for reaching the values you desire.

Desired	Actions Needed	Actualized
1.		
2.		
3.		
4.		
5.		
6.		

If you feed your critics, they will eventually eat you and complain about your taste.

- JOHN NUZZO

STRENGTH

My Bros Aren't Happy

As he lay asleep one evening, Joseph's senses seemed to hurry behind his eyes.

His dream was taking him to a new level in life, one in which his brothers bowed before him. Awakening in wonder, he was eager to share his dream with his family.

Sibling rivalry is natural, but Joseph's brothers were beyond fraternal antics; put lightly, they hated Joseph, and his dreams weren't winning over their hearts and minds (Genesis 37:8).

His brothers' hatred boiled over in a murder plot.

They maliciously
knocked him into a pit
from which he could not escape,
but instead of murdering him,
they sold him
into slavery.

Trolls and Trials

You probably won't have people despise you enough to plot your death, but you will have your haters.

Can you imagine the trolling that would have happened on Joseph's social media feeds?

Rest assured,
critics will attack
your dream.

They may attempt to make you question your purpose. It's a fact of life in carrying a dream.

Some will hate you
because your dream
seems threatening to them.

Others will hate you
because your drive
prods the unlived dreams in their lives.

It's hard to shake off the cutting remarks and, at times, calculated attacks of others. You must determine early on not to sacrifice your dream at the altar of your critics.

Your purpose is too essential
to let the haters of life
rob you from
walking out your destiny.

The trolls of life will try your commitment to the dream, and while it may not seem like much of a gift in the moment,
they are
fortifying a resolve
that is key to your success.

I Can't Come Down

The book of Nehemiah tells the story of a man who overcame the odds stacked against him.

Nehemiah was the cupbearer to the king of Persia when he got word that his homeland's walls were laid in ruins. His heart broke at the news, and he sought the king's permission to lead an expedition to rebuild the walls.

On a mission supported by the king, Nehemiah arrived at his hometown with optimism, though he met with resistance by a couple of knuckleheads named Sanballat and Tobiah who made it their mission to stop Nehemiah.

We can liken this story to what we face when we begin walking in our purpose today. When you step out to fulfill the divine dream God placed in you, the opposition will arise. The enemy doesn't attack his own, nor does he attack the complacent. He attacks those on mission and destiny.

It should come as no surprise that the enemy will launch attacks meant to discourage and distract you from fulfilling God's purpose in your life. If you fulfill what God has for you, it robs the enemy of glory.

Nehemiah didn't let anything shake him from his mission. In one scene, his enemies conspired to murder him by luring him away from his work on the walls. His reply is an invaluable reminder of the importance of dedication:

"I realized they were plotting to harm me, so I replied by sending this message to them: 'I am engaged in a great work, so I can't come. Why should I stop working to come and meet with you?'" (Nehemiah 6:2-3, NLT).

Never delay your pursuit of God to respond to your critics. Resolve in your heart to keep moving forward.

Identity

Your strength comes
from knowing
who you are—
your true identity
in Christ.

During one encounter with His critics, Jesus's identity
was assaulted by others' taunts calling for proof. The
people demanded to see signs and miracles that
would prove Jesus was who He said He was. For
most, the natural impulse would be defensive
maneuvering.

Jesus's response, though simply stated, was
profound: "These claims are valid even though I
make them about myself. For I know where I came
from and where I am going, but you don't know this
about me" (John 8:14, NLT).

Jesus didn't have anything to prove to anybody. The
need for approval did not bind him. He was 100
percent secure in who He was and is.

How different would our lives be
if we could wholeheartedly
respond to our critics,
"I know where I came from,
and I know where I'm going"?

The foundation of this view of self would require a shift in our understanding of the source of our identity.

We often mask our identity in accomplishments, possessions, and opinions.

- Accomplishments—I am what I do.

- Possessions—I am what I have.

- Opinions—I am what others think.

Too many people spend their entire lives as prisoners to the opinions of others. As the book of Proverbs claims, "Fearing people is a dangerous trap, but trusting the Lord means safety" (Proverbs 29:25, NLT).

What or who are you allowing to shape your sense of value and worth?

A Masterpiece

The truth is that you are who God says you are. We have to let that truth settle in our hearts.

You are a new creation in Christ.

You are the beloved of God.

You are a joint heir with Christ.

You are seated in heavenly places.

You are a child of the king.

You are an image-bearer: "In the image of God he created them; male and female he created them" (Genesis 1:27, NLT).

Who are you?

You are who God says you are.

God alone is the author and giver of life.

And He alone defines you.

Before you took your first breath, He had a plan in mind for you, and He placed you at this moment in time to move His mission forward: "For we are God's masterpiece. He has created us anew in Christ Jesus, so we can do the good things he planned for us long ago" (Ephesians 2:10, NLT).

The actions of your life emerge from the source of who you are.

You were created in His image—a masterpiece!

See yourself as God sees you and be free.

Free to be you.

Free to pursue your dream.

Free to change your world.

You Need a Plan

Sometimes we think of goal setting as merely a tool for task management, but there's more to it. Nehemiah was able to maintain his focus because he had a well-developed plan.

Similarly, our goals can serve as an anchor in trying times.

The best-laid plans begin with the reasoning of why.

Why is this a goal in my life,
and what will it add to my mission?

Answering this question prioritizes our resolutions during the intense times when we want to throw in the towel and walk away.

It is this question and its answer that bring us back to the center.

The next step is to set a due date. As simple as it sounds, most of us won't finish a project until the pressure of a deadline is set. To this end, I encourage you to find someone who can hold you accountable to your timeline. Identify a fellow brother or sister in Christ whom you can trust. Set regular check-in times together to evaluate your progress.

Having an accountability partner alongside you on your journey can have a make-or-break difference!

Lastly, what does victory look like? This step forces you to be realistic and specific in your goal setting.

For instance, say your goal is to have a better attitude. What does victory look like in this goal? It's hard to define because it's less of a goal and more of a value.

A realistic goal would be more along these lines: Tomorrow, I will commit to verbally appreciating one person I come across, writing one letter to someone who has impacted my life, and journaling one thing I am grateful for at the end of the day. This measurable and realistic goal reinforces the value I'm longing for in having a better attitude.

In the end, our goals help us remember what we are fighting for.

Exercise: Goal Setting

List three important goals you desire to attain in the first column.

Write down what drives you to accomplish those objectives, answering the "why" behind your goals.

Write the date you want to complete it by. Remember, without a deadline, it's not a goal.

Write out how you will know what victory looks like and how you plan on celebrating your win.

Goal	Benefit	Schedule	Victory
1.			
2.			
3.			

Gratitude changes your perspective
about life. You see the future,
experiences the present, and remember
the past in a dramatically different way.

- ERWIN RAPHAEL MCMANUS

VISION

Hold On

Joseph held his dream close to his heart and never let his circumstances deprive him of it.

Commitment to a vision demands
a perspective shift on the things of life.

You will face unfair moments,
dilemmas you may desire to wish away,
but you are here now.

Joseph could have spent the rest of his life feeling sorry for himself. In essence, he could have risen from the pit physically while being bound by the pit emotionally for the remainder of his life.

What was it about this young man that never wavered in the resolve for greatness? Vision: "Where there is no vision [no redemptive revelation of God], the people perish" (Proverbs 29:18, AMPC).

There is greatness in you waiting to be born.

As God unfolds His plan for your life, it's imperative that you remind yourself that you were created for great things.

Life will try its best to kick that truth out of you.

The ways of this world are contrary to the ways of God, and as you walk along your destined path, you will feel the pressure.

It's why the vision must be central to the plan.

Vision

When we speak of vision, imagery of eyesight comes to mind.

Sitting in the chair, hunched over, chin resting on a weird contraption, with the eye doctor all in your personal space, you hear, "Better now or now? Better one or better two?"

What's she looking for?

She aims to determine both
what you can see and
what you cannot see.

Such is also true about vision in our lives. It is as much about what we can see as it is about what we cannot see.

Open Our Eyes

Let's look at a story found in the book of 2 Kings. Israel is at war. At every turn, the enemy is baffled by Israel's ability to maneuver strategically before an attack. It was as if Israel were sitting in the war room listening to the plans.

Questions of spies in the ranks consumed the Aramean king. You can imagine his frustration and shock upon hearing the report that the prophet Elisha was disclosing his tactics (2 Kings 6:11-12).

The king's failure was not a result of a traitor in his ranks. It was the hand of God moving in the life of Elisha, showing him what lay ahead.

Enraged, the king sent an entire army to kill Elisha.

As the sun began to rise, a servant of Elisha was out and about when he discovered the army ready to rain down upon Elisha. Frightened, he hurried to the prophet to warn him of the terrible fate that awaited them all, but the news did not disturb Elisha. Confidently, he responded that those on their side were greater than the army they were up against.

Had the servant missed something?

He saw the army prepared against them, but there was no army ready to stand with them.

Had Elisha lost his mind?

Clearly, anyone can see that there was no hope of escape, let alone a victory.

Now listen to the prayer of the prophet: "'O Lord, open his eyes and let him see!' The Lord opened the young man's eyes, and when he looked up, he saw that the hillside around Elisha was filled with horses and chariots of fire" (2 Kings 6:17, NLT).

He saw what, at first, he could not see;
he was gazing at what the prophet had
seen the whole time.

No wonder Elisha was unmoved by the threat. He saw an army on his side, and then his prayer continued: "As the Aramean army advanced toward him, Elisha prayed, 'O Lord, please make them blind.' So the Lord struck them with blindness as Elisha had asked" (2 Kings 6:13-18, NLT).

The determining factor on the battlefield that day was all about vision.

Can you see the God that is on your side?

He wants to bring your dream to life even more than you do.

When you face adversity in your calling,
remind yourself that you have already won the victory because "the Spirit who lives in you is greater than the spirit who lives in the world" (1 John 4:4, NLT).

The Greater One
lives inside of you
and is determined
to see greatness
emerge from you.

Thanksgiving

The key to keeping vision is a perspective change toward gratitude.

I heard a story once about a man who was never content. He spent his life striving for more, but a gnawing voice would tell him it wasn't enough anytime he got what he desired. At the end of the man's life, he lay dying in bed when he heard the familiar voice that had taken joy from him his whole life. Spent, the man cried out,

"What now? What will you take from me?"

Eerily the voice replied, "Today, I will take nothing, for I have taken everything from you long ago."

Contentment holds on to that which can only be taken if you release it—the joy of gratitude.

Never yield your gratitude to pain.

While we cannot choose every situation that we will face in this life, we can choose how we will respond and react to life situations.

A famous biblical passage is often placed on shirts, bumper stickers, and loads of other Christian swag: "For I can do everything through Christ, who gives me strength" (Philippians 4:13, NLT).

It is a powerful statement.

But how does Paul arrive at this declaration?

He writes the book of Philippians from a prison cell, of all places, while waiting for a possible death sentence. Yet in the middle of all his suffering, he writes this beautiful letter of encouragement to a church in Philippi.

The strength of verse thirteen emerges from his resolve. Read his words: "Not that I was ever in need, for I have learned how to be content with whatever I have. I know how to live on almost nothing or with everything. I have learned the secret of living in every situation, whether it is with a full stomach or empty, with plenty or little. For I can do everything through Christ, who gives me strength" (Philippians 4:11-13, NLT).

What was his secret?

He knew how to be content.

Where do you find yourself today?

Maybe you are riding high from a victory you just won.

Or maybe you are in one of the lowest places in your life, looking up from the bottom of a pit.

Don't relinquish the vision God has given you that prompted your calling.

Hold on to it with gratitude.

Be The One

Leprosy during the time of Jesus was a disease that took more from its victims than life.

Ravaging the body and slowly killing it, leprosy caused a person to be ostracized from their community, home, and family.

Declared unclean,
the afflicted were
left to die alone.

One day, as Jesus was on His way to Jerusalem, he heard the cries of ten men dying from this horrific disease. Moved with compassion, He healed them all.

Their disease was gone.

However, like so many, these men would have lost limbs in the battle with this disease.

The disease was gone,
but the aftermath remained.

They could return to life, but it wasn't the same, as scars bore witness to their suffering.

All of them ran immediately back to their families and lives . . . except for one. After receiving a clean bill of health, one of the men hurried back to Jesus.

Falling at His feet, the man thanked the One who healed him. Jesus responded to him with these words: "Stand up and go. Your faith has healed you" (Luke 17:19, NLT).

At first glance, the story seems a bit confusing. How is it that the man is healed and then healed again?

Double healing—is that even a thing?
You see, for all ten that the ravaging of the disease
was stopped—no more loss—but for the one that
returned, there was something more.

Limbs were restored.

He was made whole again.

His gratitude
restored to him
all that was stolen
from him.

Exercise: Gratitude

In this exercise, we are leveling up our attitude of gratitude. Below is a chart; fill out three things you are thankful for today and how they added value to your life.

I am thankful for...	It added to my life by...
1.	
2.	
3.	

Your greatest regret at the end of your life will be the lions you didn't chase. You will look back longingly on risks not taken, opportunities not seized, and dreams not pursued. Stop running away from what scares you most and start chasing the God-ordained opportunities that cross your path.

- MARK BATTERSON

PITS

Pain

Suffering is the last thing you want to think of when you're in hot pursuit of your dreams,
but with the dream comes pain.

Joseph's suffering didn't begin at the hands of a stranger. It started with his own brothers.

How could they break the sacred bonds of family?

Looking up from the bottom of the pit his brothers cast him into, these questions had to flood Joseph's mind (Genesis 37:23-24).

How will you handle the pain?

Will it break you
or propel you forward?

Grit

Grit is the tenacity
that looks suffering in the eyes
and says, "Pain will not stop me."

Every pit you face in life is a test of your endurance. You can either allow them to build new strength in you or crush you, but the choice is always yours: "Dear brothers and sisters, when troubles of any kind come your way, consider it an opportunity for great joy. For you know that when your faith is tested, your endurance has a chance to grow. So let it grow, for when your endurance is fully developed, you will be perfect and complete, needing nothing" (James 1:2-4, NLT).

The scriptures are filled with stories of people who had to overcome insurmountable odds with grit and determination.

During my time at college, our president had a phrase he would repeat religiously and engrain in the student body. Kenneth W. Hagin would say,

"I cannot be defeated, and I will not quit!"

A simple statement that captures the attitude of grit.

I Cannot Be Defeated

Remember that you are on a mission for God. You are living out the dream He placed in your heart. With that in mind, there is nothing that you are up against that can or will defeat you. I know that's a bold statement, but unless we get it settled, there will be a level of defeated thinking that will try to dominate your thoughts somewhere in the back of your mind.

No matter how big the obstacles seem,
you serve the God of the impossible (Matthew 19:26).

What's more, even if you fall, it's not over:

"The godly may trip seven times, but they will get up again. But one disaster is enough to overthrow the wicked" (Proverbs 24:16, NLT).

Grit is the attitude that looks up from the bottom of the pit and says,

"I'm not helpless!
This is but one part of my life,
a footnote in a long story that
will not rob my destiny.
If anything,
like a rock in a slingshot,
it will propel me forward!"

I Will Not Quit

Here is where the real test of grit resides:
in the determination not to quit.

Every trial we face will pass.

Sometimes we conclude that the temporary circumstances will last forever.

The danger in this type of thinking is the loss of hope,
but as the psalmist promises us,

"Weeping may
last through the night,
but joy comes
with the morning"
(Psalm 30:5, NLT).

We do not deny the pain of the pit.

We are, however, denying the pit victory.

Determine:

I will not stop.

I will not back down.

I will not give up.

I will not abandon hope.

I will not throw in the towel.

I will not quit.

My Mule's in a Pit

I heard a story about an old mule that fell into an abandoned well. At the bottom of the well, the poor mule brayed with all his might, hoping to get the attention of his owner. Hearing all the commotion, the farmer rushed about looking for the old mule. The scene of the frightened beast disheartened him. Working late into the evening, the farmer tried every solution he could think of to rescue the poor mule before calling it a night.

It was a lonely evening for the mule as he gazed up at the stars, trying to resolve himself to the inevitable fate that awaited him. The next day the farmer rose early, and, with the help of a nearby neighbor, they worked diligently into the afternoon trying to figure out what to do. In hopeless abandonment, the farmer concluded that their labor efforts were not worth an old mule in an abandoned well that should have been filled years ago. Trading the lasso for two shovels in his shed, the farmer and his friend began to fill the well with dirt.

The first shovel of dirt took the mule by surprise until he realized what was happening. He cried out with everything he had, hoping that the persisting farmer would stop, but to no avail—his shrieks didn't change what was happening. As the mule paused for a moment, a scoop of dirt hit his back. His panic turned to anger at what was happening and he violently shook the earth off. Another thought quickly interrupted his rage as the dirt from his back settled under his hooves.

He could passively allow the fate of this moment to rest in the hands of a hopeless farmer, or he could do something about his situation. As each shovel of dirt hit his back, rather than braying, he committed to shaking it off and stepping up. That which was supposed to bury him became the platform beneath his feet, inching him closer and closer to the top. Pure amazement overtook the farmer and his neighbor when the brave mule stepped over the ledge of the now filled well. He refused to die in their pit. No, with every hit meant to destroy him, he learned that if you can shake it off and step up, it's only a matter of time before you're standing at the top.

Embrace this same spirit!

Let each stone thrown
against you
serve as another platform
toward the
fulfillment of your dream!

A Grit Plan

In my high school, I remember every hallway had a glass box somewhere along the wall. On the glass, red letters read,

"In case of fire,
break the glass.
Pull the fire alarm."

When the heat gets cranked up, you need a "break the glass, pull the alarm" system established—a grit plan.

There are three essential components to a grit plan:

Help.

We were not created to live in isolation.

We need each other for the journey (Ecclesiastes 4:9-12).

Who do you have in your life that inspires you?

Motivates you?

These people in your life
won't always tell you
what you want to hear,
but they will tell you
what you need to hear
without tearing you down.

When you leave their presence, you feel charged.

Heart.

The heart speaks
to the motivation
behind your drive.

It is the "why" we discussed in chapter four.

Write it down (Habakkuk 2:2).

You need to see it
and remind yourself of it often to live it.

Saturate your
heart and mind
in your why.

When you do this daily, it will come to define your life
and you will naturally walk in it.

Hope.

We are not machines.

In the very story of our creation, God necessitates the need for rest and refreshment (Genesis 2:1-3).

What are the things in life that bring you hope?

For some, it may be a walk in the woods.

For others, it could be binge-watching your favorite series on Netflix.

Whatever the case may be, you need something that restores and refreshes you to keep you in the fight.

Exercise: A Grit Plan

Let's develop a Grit Plan. It will be your go-to guide when things get tough and you're tempted to quit.

In the "Help" column, write down names by answering this question: Who can I call on to speak truth and encouragement?

In the "Heart" column, write down your reason for pursuing your dream. When times get tough, reminding yourself of your "why" is critical.

In the "Hope" column, write down the things that refresh you. It's important to remember and do the things in life that restore hope to you.

Help	Heart	Hope

You cannot control what happens to you, but you can control your attitude toward what happens to you, and in that, you will be mastering change rather than allowing it to master you.

- BRIAN TRACY

PALACES

The Illusion of Control

After he emerged from the pit, Joseph found himself in a nice place—or so it appeared. He was working in the household of a wealthy owner and was quickly promoted to a role of leadership (Genesis 39).

Outwardly speaking,
it looked like a
great position
until you
remember that
this wasn't employment;
it was slavery.

In a few verses, Joseph's story goes from a divine vision of greatness to slavery in a palatial home. He was in the environment he had seen for himself, but everything around him wasn't his, including his own life.

We long for the idea of control in every area of life, as it affords a sense of security.

The reality is that there are many things in life beyond our control, and the sooner we embrace that concept, the more quickly we are able to focus on what we can control and master that.

Joseph could not control what he wore,
the position he held,
the food he ate,
or even where he laid his head at night,
but he could control his character.

No matter what he stood against, he remained steadfast in his faith. Nothing could break the foundation that Joseph had in the Lord.

His master's wife lusted after Joseph and on many occasions attempted to seduce him into an affair. In every case, Joseph maintained his integrity. Everything came to a head one day when she attempted to force herself on Joseph, who tore away. Clutching his cloak in her hands as he fled and insulted by his rejection, she ran to her husband, accusing Joseph of attacking her. Having no control over his fate, Joseph was sent to prison on the baseless lie of his assailant.

There will be times in life when we face baseless persecution ourselves, even when we do the right thing in response.

Let Joseph's story serve as inspiration to hold tightly to your character, for it will ultimately take you precisely where God has called you.

Walking by Faith

"For we live by
believing and not by seeing"
(2 Corinthians 5:7, NLT).

This is a small verse that packs a great punch. Is it true of our lives? Or would the verse of our life more accurately read,

"For we live by
the illusion of control?"

Speaking of faith is far easier than walking it out.

It reminds me of Israel's wandering experience. In a period in between the pain and the promise, they traveled in a land where they had no control. From the navigational direction they followed (Numbers 9:15:23) to the very food they ate (Exodus 16:15-20), everything was beyond their control.

They did not have a three-year master plan detailing every move. They were given just enough for each day.

The truth of the matter is that
there are many unknowns
you will face tomorrow,
things that will be far
beyond your control.

We all struggle with the desire for instant gratification, for an exception to the plan,
for control,
but we are not promised any of these in life.

Can you trust that the God who has led you thus far will not let you down now?

Paradox

There are many things that baffle me in life.

Why is it that when I'm in a rush to get somewhere, I can't find anything—keys, wallet, phone?

Why is it that the more I try to not think about something, the more I do?

Why is it that my sleepless night of stressing over the project seems to only make things worse the next morning?

Control can have a paradoxical nature to it.

At times, the very things we attempt to exercise the most control over become the things we have little to no control over, and as a result, we are left with anxiety that eats at the core of our being.

Consider the question of Jesus: "Can all your worries add a single moment to your life?" (Matthew 6:27, NLT).

The honest answer to His question is that worry hasn't added anything, but it has taken much:

Sleep.

Peace.

Health.

Relationships.

All worry will do is steal from all these areas of your life!

Paul's Equation

In chapter five we looked at a few verses from Paul's letter to the Philippians, written while he was in prison. I think it's important to keep in mind the setting he is in when we look at what he wrote concerning worry:

"Don't worry about anything; instead, pray about everything. Tell God what you need, and thank him for all he has done. Then you will experience God's peace, which exceeds anything we can understand. His peace will guard your hearts and minds as you live in Christ Jesus" (Philippians 4:6-7, NLT).

Again, here is a man in a predicament that would leave most in despair. Yet his fixation is resting upon the unknowns. In fact, he seems to show little care for what most would be concerned with.

I want you to see the equation Paul gives us for leaving worry behind and living in peace:

Prayer + Gratitude = Peace

Paul's theology lends way to a path of peace that is found in laying everything before God and giving thanks for what we do have in life.

In the Garden

How do we lay everything before God?

It requires the embrace of trust amid the unknown; trust that God's plan is far greater than our own and that He will provide.

When Jesus was in the Garden of Gethsemane, when He would soon lay down His life for us all, He prayed these powerful words:
"My Father! If it is possible, let this cup of suffering be taken away from me. Yet I want your will to be done, not mine" (Matthew 26:39, NLT).

Here, at the moment when His purpose was soon to be fulfilled, Jesus began to struggle the hardest. This is common. When we are close to the fruition of our dream is when things often become hardest.

But look again how Jesus responds. The words of our Savior, in the middle of His greatest trial, were,
"Not my will, but Yours be done."

And it was with His final words on the cross that He says, "Father, I entrust my spirit into your hands" (Luke 23:46, NLT).

These verses show us exactly what we need to do in the time of our greatest trials: to release all our fear, anxiety, and pain into God's hands.

Even when everything is making us feel as if we want to quit, we need to put God's will above our own and accept His strength. That's what Jesus did, and that's what we are called to do also.

Trust

My wife's favorite author is Corrie ten Boom. As the Nazis invaded her homeland in the Netherlands during World War II, Corrie and her family hid Jewish people in their home, helping hundreds escape the reach of the gas chambers. Her family paid a great price for their efforts; her father and sister both lost their lives in prison, and Corrie was the only survivor.

In our kitchen sits a plaque with a quote by Corrie:

"Never be afraid to trust an unknown future to a known God."

God can be trusted with the unknowns.

You don't have to spend your life in an anxious knot, desperately trying to make the dream happen on your own.

He is with you, guiding and directing in the places where we don't have control.

Exercise: Control

When setting goals and vision for your life, there are controllable and uncontrollable aspects to remember.

This exercise will help you know your part and what you need to surrender to God in trust.

Things to keep in mind as you do this exercise:

1. You cannot control others, their thoughts, actions, reactions, opinions, etc.
2. Many circumstances and events are beyond our control like the loss of a job, accidents, etc.
3. You CAN control your attitude, outlook, actions, and responses to your environment.

Want	Need	Can Control	Cannot Control

The paradox of faith is that when we conform our lives to Christ then we gain our true freedom. And its fruit is profound and lasting happiness.

- VINCENT NICHOLS

PRISONS

Rock Bottom

The miserable stench of the dark hollows of prison and the unrelenting sounds of chains would have broken most people. Here sat Joseph, the once-celebrated son of a doting father, the former manager of a wealthy estate owner, now stripped of dignity and any semblance of success.

And for what?

Holding firm to his values.

If ever there was an understandable time to throw in the towel, now would be it.

Prisons are dark places.

Different than pits, for at least in pits you can see your way up.

Your dream will face prison moments. Moments when you can see no way up, no way out. Now is not the time to lose hope.

Put into practice what you have gained along the way.

Your integrity.

Your inner strength.

Your resolve.

Your grit.

Your faith.

Like the pit, you will emerge from this prison.
But while you are here,
what can you gain?

Joseph made the most out of every situation he found himself in, and the prison was no exception.

He put his skill of interpreting dreams to practice, and his faithfulness in the darkest place of his life opened the door for his dream to come to pass. Two years later, this act of interpreting a dream would be remembered and lead Joseph to the fulfillment of his dreams.

Hope

You cannot afford to lose hope.
Hope is the voice that reminds you,

even in the darkest of moments,
that things will get better.

The struggle is real. I know it can be hard to believe things will change when you find yourself in a prison, but they will.

Consider that this moment, too, will pass.

One of the phrases that makes my skin crawl is, "It is what it is." Usually, it is spoken from the lips of someone who has surrendered to the lie that the temporary is unmovable.

In the previous chapter, we talked about how relinquishing control to God is essential in pursuing a dream. However, relinquishing control is different than abandoning hope.

The former says, "God, I know you are going to see me through this, and in the end, we will win!"
The latter says, "God, not even you can fix this mess."

Faith Brings Giants

I've met people throughout my life who have told me they never struggled with discouragement a day in their lives. I'm not saying they're lying, but if you're going to live a God-sized dream in your life, there will be battles with discouragement along the way. Perhaps the lack of a struggle directly correlates to the illusion of control and safe living.

People of faith have giants to slay and mountains to move that bring bouts with discouragement. For example, there are so many who pour all of their blood, sweat, and tears into their ministry only to find little or no growth. I've known many people who have endured this for years. They operate their ministry in a place that desperately needs the Gospel, and they are trying everything they can to reach the people there with it, but to no avail and through no fault of their own. Sometimes our missions seem impossible.

These kinds of situations bring about great discouragement in our hearts.

It's hard to give everything we have and not see the fruits of our labor!

But I assure you, the fruit will come.

When you plant a tree, does it grow overnight? No, it doesn't. It takes years and years for that tree to become full, vibrant, and mature. It's the same way with the seeds we plant in our ministries. While we don't always see the fruit of our work right away, rest assured that God has a plan, and the seeds you plant will bloom in ways you could never have imagined.

Even Elijah

One of the greatest prophets of the Old Testament was Elijah, who himself had to fend off discouragement. To set the scene of his lament, we first need to witness the roller coaster of emotions experienced.

God sent word through Elijah that a severe drought was imminent and that Elijah was to hide out by a brook (1 Kings 17:1-5). When the drought hit the land, God supernaturally provided nourishment, with food delivered to Elijah by a raven and water from the brook.

A few verses later, God told Elijah to visit the house of a widow. Not knowing the dire straits the woman was in, Elijah asked for something to eat upon his arrival. Broken by the prospect of starvation, the widow explained the scarcity of her resources and how she was preparing the last meal for her and her son before they yielded to the fate of death. This was not a chance encounter for Elijah; God had sent him there to minister. He instructed the woman to make her meal and promised that God would provide. With every meal, God refilled the containers of flour and oil so that the house never went hungry again (1 Kings 17:8-16).

Some time later, the woman's son became ill and died. Elijah prayed for the young man, and he came back to life (1 Kings 17:17-24).

From the widow's home, Elijah was led by the Lord to inform the king that the drought was about to come to an end.

When he arrived at Mount Carmel, he laid a challenge out before the prophets of the false god Baal. He told them that each side should prepare an altar and sacrifice, and whichever god answered their prayer by consuming their sacrifice should be understood to be the one true God. The prophets of Baal consented to the challenge (1 Kings 18:22-24). After crying, pleading, and begging for Baal to answer, they saw no change upon the altar they built (1 Kings 18:26-29).

Elijah stepped forward, dug a trench around his altar, doused the sacrifice, and filled the trench with water.

He then prayed, and God sent fire from heaven that consumed the sacrifice and even the altar's rocks (1 Kings 18:30-39).

Elijah then seized the 450 prophets of Baal and killed them (1 Kings 18:40).

Continuing in his assignment to inform the king, Elijah settled upon a mountain and began to pray. He sent a servant out to inspect the sky for signs of rain. The servant returned and informed Elijah that he had seen nothing. Six times the servant went out, and with each inspection, the report was the same. On the seventh run at the same scene, the servant came back with a dismal report. He saw a cloud, but it was only about the size of a man's fist. Elijah instructed the servant to hurry to the king and inform him to get in his chariot and leave, for an abundance of rain was coming (1 Kings 18:41-45).

Fleeing from the storm, the king's chariot raced ahead, but God gave Elijah supernatural strength, and he outran the king's horse and chariot (1 Kings 18:46).

If you had just experienced everything Elijah did throughout these few chapters, you would think there would be nothing that could intimidate or discourage you, but that was not the case.

Upon hearing the news that Elijah had seized Queen Jezebel's prophets, she became furious. She sent word to Elijah that she was going to see him dead. Fearing for his life, Elijah was on the run. Resting under a tree, he prayed, "I have had enough, Lord. Take my life, for I am no better than my ancestors who have already died" (1 Kings 19:4).

In Elijah's story, we see one of the most revered biblical figures struggle with discouragement.

How does this guy go from these amazing experiences to the dark place of despair?

Let me ask you this: if even Elijah was subject to the discouragement that we can experience in our faith, do you really believe that we would be spared that same struggle?

Discouragement

It hits us all,
and just as we witnessed in the life of Elijah, even if you're coming off high moments with God, you can

still have a dark prison moment that makes you want to walk away from it all.

So, how do you overcome it?

To begin, you have to change your outlook. It brings us back to the principle of gratitude:

"Be thankful in all circumstances, for this is God's will for you who belong to Christ Jesus" (1 Thessalonians 5:18, NLT).

Notice Paul didn't say be thankful "for" all but "in" all.

What he's telling us is that no matter what you are walking through, you can find something in your life to be thankful for.

This brings me to the second point in breaking discouragement: change your speech.

That's tough, I know. Especially if your prison involves having an injustice done to you like Joseph—trust me on this one—bitterness will only keep you trapped longer. We will come back to this point in the next chapter.

Even if you find yourself in a prison you didn't create, serving a sentence that isn't yours, and left abandoned by those you trusted, remember God will get you through. And while He's working, your mind and words must be fixed on hope and not despair.

Dare to Hope

"The thought of my suffering and homelessness is bitter beyond words. I will never forget this awful time, as I grieve over my loss. Yet I still dare to hope when I remember this: The faithful love of the Lord never ends! His mercies never cease" (Lamentations 3:19-22, NLT).

Jeremiah is not diminishing the pain he walked through. He is, however, determined that his suffering will not be the final word. The plan locked inside of him was too big to give up on.

He dared to hope again.

Even in the darkest of moments, refuse to give up.

Keep hope when it seems too far gone.

Keep hope when you're tired and want to quit.

Keep hope when it seems like you're alone.

Prisons are trying, but there's a big dream inside of you still. And as long as you're breathing, there's still work to be done.

I dare you to hope.

Exercise: Prison Reflections

Consider a time in your life when you thought all hope was lost.

What lessons did you learn in the dark season of your life?

_____

_____

_____

_____

_____

_____

How did it make you stronger?

_____

_____

_____

_____

_____

_____

If going back and changing it would make you a different person than you are now, would you do it? Why?

_____

_____

_____

_____

_____

_____

_____

_____

If you can't figure out your purpose,
figure out your passion. For your passion
will lead you right into your purpose.

- T.D. JAKES

PASSION

The Forge

From his darkest days, Joseph's faithfulness loosened the chains of bondage and elevated him to a place of honor. His dream was finally coming to pass.

Joseph faced what every dreamer will encounter. Dreams arise within our hearts as we face the struggles of life.

These trials will test our dreams' resolve!

But if the dreamer doesn't quit and embraces the lessons learned along the way, they will persevere and see the fulfillment of their dream.

God will equip them along the way, taking away any distractions and leaving only what is necessary to fulfill the mission before them.

Purpose

At the core of us all is the burning desire to answer the question, "Why am I here?"

When you discover your purpose in life, you discover the thing that causes you to wake up and keep going.

I heard a story told of a rich man visiting Mother Teresa of Calcutta. When he arrived, he found her changing the wound bandages of a man devastated by disease.

Disgusted at the sight, the rich man exclaimed, "You couldn't pay me all the money in the world to do that." Without missing a beat, Mother Teresa replied, "You couldn't pay me to do it either."

God longs to take your past, gifts, talents, and passion and use them to change the world.

Past

Your present tells the story of your past.

All you have been through, in both the good times and the bad, have worked together to create the canvas on which you can now lay out the brushstrokes of your dream.

Jesus has given you a clean slate in which to write your story, using everything God has taught you from both the good and bad you've experienced throughout your life.

For me, my life began in
struggle, suffering, and abuse.

I will never forget the Sunday morning in 1997 when I surrendered my brokenness to Jesus and experienced true life.

It was Jesus who took the tattered pieces of my past and wove a tapestry of purpose from the pain; from the adversity and suffering, a drive to help others reach beyond their pain was birthed.

I have come to discover that our pasts can be a gift or a stumbling block toward our destiny.

The choice is ours.

Make your past
a platform
for your dream
to stand upon.

Personality

"For in him we live and move and exist" (Acts 17:28, NLT).

There are countless numbers of personality tests available to you on the internet and I encourage you to explore them. A few that have been well researched come to mind: the Values in Action Inventory (VIA-IS), Myers-Briggs (MBTI), and the Big Five Personality Test. Each one was created to help you discover more clearly who you are and what makes you tick. What makes your dream unique is you.

It's your
past and personality
coming together on
a mission to help others.

Passion

What are the things that excite you?

What motivates you?

What are those things that when you get involved in them, you seem to lose sense of time?

It's your passion.

You might use phrases like:
"It just feels right."
"I live for this."

Likewise, our passion can cause the most incredible pain in our lives when left unfulfilled or neglected.

To this end, Paul wrote,
"Fan into flames the spiritual gift God gave you" (2 Timothy 1:6, NLT).

It is up to you to take the gift He placed in you and fan it into flames. Utilize your God-given gifts and passions for the building of God's Kingdom. This is done through engaging in ministry and preaching the Word of God to everyone you meet.

Endurance

We are a living testament to the daily decisions we make. Are we making choices to fuel our passion, or are we depleting our reservoirs?

Let's look at a passage we read earlier about Jesus: "Jesus grew in wisdom and in stature and in favor with God and all the people" (Luke 2:52, NLT).

Stature speaks of a physical state.

Wisdom speaks of a mental state.

Favor with people speaks of a social state.

Favor with God speaks of a spiritual state.

If our future is to sustain a dream that will last, it must be built on a solid foundation, a foundation that tends wholistically to your being:

Physically. The physical aspect of life can often be the most overlooked. Paul speaks of our bodies as a temple to bring glory to God (1 Corinthians 6:19-20). It is hard to glorify God through a body that has been mistreated and neglected to pursue other objectives in one's life. The demands that drain the body, if not replenished, will, in turn, dampen the soul. Make your health a priority.

Mentally. Cognitive Behavioral Psychology has taught us a lot in understanding the power of our thought life, attesting to the ancient wisdom literature: "For as he thinketh in his heart, so is he" (Proverbs 23:7, KJV). Your emotions, to a great extent, will determine your actions. We must both guard and feed our thought life lest we find ourselves diverted along a detour never intended for the journey of the dream.

Socially. It was love that caused Jesus to enter our world, and it was love that caused Him to walk slowly through the crowds. We were not created to live in isolation from one another but to encounter, learn, and encourage one another. A dream that one individual can do alone is too small. Yours is a dream so big that you need the help of another to see it come to pass.

Spiritually. This life is filled with challenges that contend for our hearts; as a result, we must be proactive in designing and developing a walk that is intentional in seeking after God. Make church life, devotional time, and prayer a priority. They put us in check when we fall out of balance and pick up destructive habits and realign us to what is most important.

Exercise: Purpose

In the diagram below, list:

Three things from your past that define you.

Three strengths of your personality that support you.

Three passions that drive you.

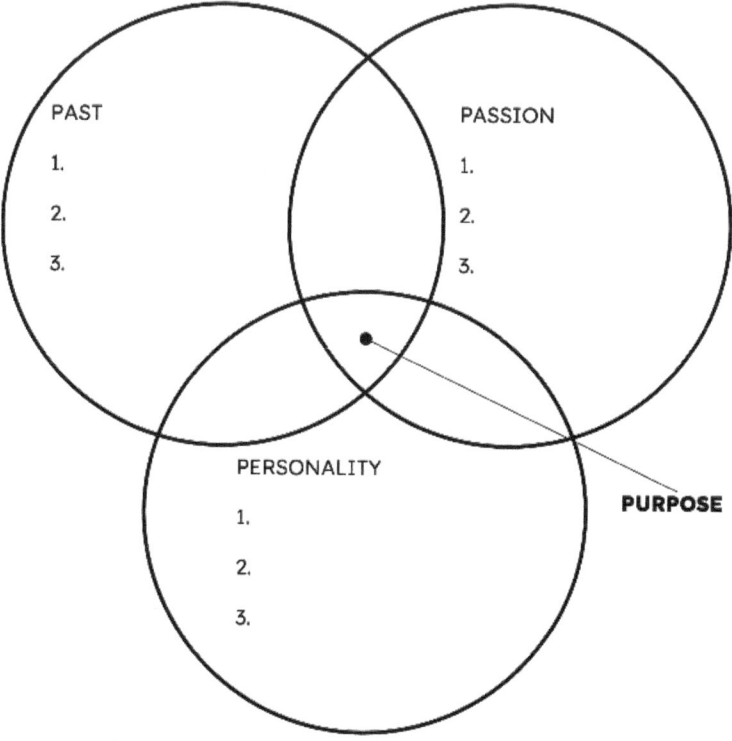

Great men are just ordinary men that
didn't quit.

- TOMMY BARNETT

PERSISTENCE

Greatness Will Come

Any time you determine in your life to do something great for God,
you will be hit with obstacles,
mountains to move,
and giants to slay.

In the end, Joseph's dream finally came to pass. Joseph ruled over Egypt for eighty years! He ruled there up until his death. Joseph had come a long way since the days of working the fields with his brothers, but those dreams God planted within him back in those days came to realization in Joseph's godly servant leadership.

His story was filled with twists and turns,
moments that were not for the faint of heart.

What we learn from Joseph is that if we are willing to hold on to a dream when everything in us wants to let go, in the end, we will see greatness come to life.

Faith

What are you calling forth in your future?
At times we shape our vision for the future according
to the hits life sends our way.
Hopeless thoughts lead to hopeless words,
and we stay stuck.

Saturate your life with
faith-filled words of
hope and
destiny (Matthew 12:35-37).

Your best days are ahead of you. Start calling your purpose out (Mark 11:23), no matter what you are facing. By speaking your purpose out into the world, you will bring about its manifestation!

Do You Want More?

One day Jesus entered Jerusalem through an entrance where many people lay sick and dying.

There was a tradition whereby the waters would bubble up, and it was thought that the first person to dive into the waters at the sign of the bubbling would be cured of whatever illness they had.

The King James Version records that here lay
the blind (without vision),
halt (without motion), and
withered (without moisture) (John 5:3).

Locking eyes with a man who had been lying there for thirty-eight years, Jesus approached him and asked a simple question:

"Would you like to get well?" (John 5:6, NLT).

At first glance, it seems a bit insulting. The man had been there for so long. You would probably assume, "Of course, he wants to get better. It's why he's there."

However, consider this man's environment. He was surrounded by those who had
lost vision,
stopped moving, and
dried up long ago.

Jesus stepped on the scene and asked the man if he was content with what he had known or if he wanted something different, something more. The man was stirred by Jesus's words, and Jesus healed him on the spot, equipping the man to walk into a new life only available through Christ.

Don't Stop Now

It can seem hard to keep going when you're holding a dream in your heart that doesn't match your present circumstances.

The quick fix can be tempting:

"Just give up."

But Paul exhorts us to keep going:

"So let's not get tired of doing what is good. At just the right time, we will reap a harvest of blessing if we don't give up" (Galatians 6:9, NLT).

Don't stop now.

You've come too far and
been through too much
to turn back now!

Well Done

It's God who placed the desire in your heart to begin with, and if you are faithful, you will see it come to pass.

Know this along the way: you are going to experience great victories, but they are never final destinations.

With each new level comes a greater revelation of just how big the dream is.

So, how will you know when you've arrived?

You will find yourself standing in the presence of overwhelming love.

Hearing the words of Jesus:

"'Well done, my good and faithful servant.
You have been faithful in handling this small amount,
so now I will give you many more responsibilities.
Let's celebrate together!'" (Matthew 25:21, NLT).

Conclusion

God has planted a dream within your heart for a reason. He did not put it there so that it would be left unfulfilled. He desires for you to walk in it!

What is your dream?

What is your purpose?

Delight yourself in His presence and discover his plan.

God loves you more than you will ever know. He envisioned you and had a plan for your life before you were ever born. Never doubt the dream He has given you. He wants nothing more than to see you accomplish it!

God will be your biggest support and ally along your journey. Put time into cultivating your relationship with Him.

Take Joseph's story to heart. As you walk in your God-given purpose, never stop dreaming.

Never quit.

Trust that if the Lord has called you to it, He will see it through to fruition. If you follow and trust in Him, He will equip you with everything you need to get it done.

Always be a dreamer.

Just as God led Joseph from humble beginnings to ruling an entire nation, so too will He lead you to a future you could never have imagined.

All you have to do is trust and walk with Him.

About Ray

Evangelist. Missionary. Author.

I know what it's like to fight for identity and the desire to find purpose, meaning, and value. I experienced the stinging pains of abuse, suffering, and lack as a child.

My past is built upon a foundation of resilience that drives me to help others reach beyond their pain.

I was born to a teenage mother of fourteen seeking solace in marriage at twelve from the horrifying abuse of her stepfather. Though she worked hard to make a life for herself and her children, her emotional scars led her into a series of abusive marriages that nearly claimed her life.

By seventeen, my life was fully a mess. I contemplated dropping out of high school, and depression was a daily struggle. Everything changed, however, when my mother surprisingly declared that she was going to go to church and wanted to know if I would go with her.

Out of curiosity, I agreed to go. As I bowed my head in prayer, I heard a voice within that said my life could be different if I surrendered. Tears welled up from somewhere deep within, and I cried, "I need a change in my life." I surrendered to the Lord, and for the first time, I felt alive.

Seeing God's power at work, I knew He called me to use my pain as a platform to minister to others. I set a new course for my family by graduating high school and then college.

I view my past through the lens of creating who I am today.

Through speaking and writing, my passion is to help others not remain a victim of their past but to become someone who can take the past, and with God's help, create a platform for their future.

TruMission.com

At TruMission.com, we know you want to experience a fulfilled life.

That is the kind of life Jesus came to give us all.

Finding someone to help you along the way can be frustrating and confusing, with so many claiming to have the answer. This can leave you settling for something less. We know what it feels like.

For over 20 years, we have helped hundreds of individuals and organizations discover their mission in life.

Here is how we do it:

1. Subscribe
Subscribe to our website and explore a vast library of books, teachings, and more designed to help you on your mission.

2. Grow
Gain the confidence you've longed for as your mission becomes clear.

3. Impact
Join us on a mission that's bigger than all of us. If you've been impacted by these powerful messages, help us take them around the world.

So, subscribe today at www.TruMission.com and be encouraged through weekly videos, resources, and opportunities that will help you discover your mission in life.

The days of feeling lost and confused will be over.

The life of purpose and mission begins today.